Minds and Motion

Active Learning for the Creative Classroom

Cally Stockton

National Middle School Association
Westerville, Ohio

Library of Congress Cataloging-in-Publication Data

Stockton, Cally.
Minds and motion: active learning for the creative classroom/Cally Stockton.
    p. cm.
ISBN 978-1-56090-242-3
1. Active learning--United States. 2. Student-centered learning. 3. Creative teaching.
I. National Middle School Association. II. Title.

LB1027.23.S66 2011
371.1--dc22

2011009135

National Middle School Association
4151 Executive Parkway, Suite 300
Westerville, Ohio 43081
1-800-528-NMSA f: 614-895-4750
www.nmsa.org

Dedication

To hardworking and compassionate educators and the students and parents
who inspire and challenge us to be the best we can be.

Acknowledgements

I would like to express my appreciation to the administrators, staff, students, and parents of Cache La Poudre Middle School for providing the environment for me to teach and try new ideas. I also value the opportunities I have received for professional development through Poudre School District and would particularly like to recognize Ben Johnson (my technology guru) and Mary Hasl (mentor coordinator and director of the teacher leadership academy). This book owes much of its existence to the encouragement of my former student teacher and now colleague and friend, Jill Brito, and to my friend and role model, John Perricone (author of Zen and the Art of Public School Teaching). I would also like to thank the editorial staff at NMSA for their excellent communication, attention to detail, and expertise in guiding this book through publication.

Thank you to my parents, sisters, other family members, and friends for their support and encouragement. I especially want to thank my husband, Ken, and daughter, Ruth, for all their listening, laughter, and love.

About the Author

Cally Stockton teaches Spanish and Skills for Adolescents at Cache La Poudre Middle School in LaPorte, Colorado. Before becoming a public school teacher, she held several administrative and teaching positions including director of a job training program for inner-city youth, hospital department manager, and management trainer and consultant. Cally earned a bachelor's degree in psychology from the University of Indianapolis, a bachelor's degree in foreign language and literature from Colorado State University, and a master's degree in American studies from the University of Maryland.

Cally has presented some of the book activities at National Middle School Association's 2010 Annual Conference in Baltimore and has been a guest speaker for the teacher licensure program at Colorado State University. For more information on Cally's current writing and speaking activities or to invite her to lead training at your school, contact her at teacher.cally@gmail.com

Table of Contents

Introduction vii

Name Games 1

    Name Snake 5

    Name Juggle 6

    Name Tarp Tag 7

    Four Corners 8

    Name Association Games 9

    Heads Up, Seven Up 10

    Names Count 11

    Play My Name 12

Getting Better Acquainted 15

    Two Truths and a Lie 17

    Paired Venn Diagram 18

    Human Shuffle 19

    People Bingo 20

    Vote with Your Feet 22

    Backward name (Ym Eman Si) 23

Warm-Ups and Attention-Getters 25

    If You Can Hear Me 27

    Finish the Phrase 28

Basta 29

Alphabattle 30

Amazing Math 31

Memory Test 32

Anagrams 33

Mental Vacation 34

On the Edge 35

Pendulum Predictor 36

What Do You See? 37

Tell and Draw 42

Teambuilding, Teamwork and Collaborative Learning 47

Class Constitution 49

Class Flag or Coat of Arms 50

Class Fight Song 51

Circle-Up Activities 52

Simple Relays 53

Tallest Tower 54

Balloon Volleyball and Balloon Relay 55

Beanbag Toss 56

Mind Field 57

Flying Carpet or Flyer Saucer Relay 58

Pirate Pick Up 59

How Many Uses? 60

The Judge 61

Memory Match 62

Rock, Paper, Scissors Variations 63

Story Cards 64

Who Am I? 65

Resources and Suggested Reading 67

Introduction

When I tell someone that I am a middle school teacher, I usually get one of two reactions: "You must be a saint" or "You must be crazy." It does take a lot of patience to teach this age group, and it helps to have a sense of humor and some creativity. Most of all, you need to enjoy your work so that the students will enjoy learning. Boredom is contagious, but so is enthusiasm.

If you are a middle school teacher, youth group leader, or someone else with the privilege of working with young adolescents, you know that young people between the ages of 10 and 15 need activity and variety to channel their energy in a positive direction. A diverse and dynamic group, they all are going through many important physical, social, emotional, and cognitive changes. Although they need structure and clear directions (usually repeated several times), they also want opportunities to practice independence and show leadership.

Students, from elementary age to adult learners, learn best when the activity—whether lecture, group work, or hands-on practice—is divided into shorter blocks of time. In my experience, the average attention span for middle grades students (how long they can focus without some kind of change in position or activity) is between 10 and 20 minutes, so I designed all of the activities in this book to be done in that length of time. Shorter variations of the activities can serve as quick warm-ups or fill those five-minute gaps at the ends of classes. Combining different variations creates a series of activities useful for longer time spans.

How to use the activities. Although they may seem simple, these activities can be the starting point or vehicle for powerful learning. For example, Vote with Your Feet, an activity in the Getting Better Acquainted section, can show the range of diversity in the types of music students like and can show that global warming may be "hot" topic for science this year. In this activity, students physically plant themselves on a spectrum that shows their positions on a variety of topics. What might students learn about themselves and others if, after studying a unit, they actually moved to a different spot on the continuum? What kinds of multiple intelligences/learning styles would be tapped if, while standing in place along the continuum, the class made a one-dimensional bar graph on paper representing the

3-D bar graph their bodies were making? A social studies activity could involve role playing a real issue confronting the UN, Congress, or state legislators or a class issue for which there are differing viewpoints. This simple activity can help students begin to understand the complexity of reaching compromise to achieve goals (a balanced budget for Congress, a lunch menu for the class party).

Use these simple activities to warm up, to understand prior knowledge, to introduce lessons, to model processes at work in the students' worlds—the kids will love them, and you will infuse your classes with energy. Motivated, enthusiastic students create fewer class management problems and engage in powerful, long-lasting learning.

Origin of activities. Just like good recipes, many of these activities have been around for a long time. I have collected them over the years in my various roles as a psychology student, youth worker, management trainer, school volunteer, parent, and teacher. The games in the book are part of the public domain, and I have provided clear instructions and suggestions for variations that will encourage your own creativity.

Tested and approved by hundreds of middle grades students, the activities have low physical risk and are cognitively, socially, and emotionally appropriate for young adolescents. (Disclaimer: Anyone who works with middle grades students knows that without proper supervision, they can turn paper folding into a full-contact sport.)

Book organization. The activities are divided into four sections—Name Games; Getting Better Acquainted; Warm-Ups and Attention-Getters; and Teambuilding, Teamwork, and Collaborative Learning. The activities include the following information:

- Number of people gives the range of group sizes appropriate for each activity.
- Time gives approximate time length for each activity and often provides a suggestion about when to use it.
- Materials are easily obtainable and inexpensive; this section also details whether the activity is suitable for outdoors or indoors and whether desks or tables are needed.
- Directions are step-by-step and based on what has worked best in the classroom.
- Teaching Points suggest discussion questions, topic connections, and reflection strategies.
- Variations suggest ways to connect to various content areas, adjustments to make based on available time and ways to extend the activity for increased complexity.
- Modifications suggest ways to meet challenged students' needs.
- Notes provide troubleshooting support based on observations of the activity in the classroom.

Having clear instructions and materials ready avoids losing valuable teaching time in lengthy transitions from one activity to another. In fact, once students have learned how to do a particular activity, they will transition quickly and can even lead the games. Depending on how and when they are used, the activities can serve many purposes, from learning names to developing higher-order thinking skills. I hope that you and your students will enjoy these activities and that some will become regular traditions in your classroom.

Name Games

My goal is to learn all of my students' names (125 to 150) within the first two or three class periods of the school year. This is the first step in making a connection with each student to best meet his or her needs during the year. The name games help you know the students as individuals—their interests, their backgrounds, how they relate to others—to begin to gather data for differentiation. Watching the students interact, you begin evaluating their social skills, emotional issues, intellectual abilities, frustration levels, abilities to concentrate, and so on. The name games also function to establish a respectful and caring classroom environment that prevents bullying and lay the foundation for classroom management, because you can immediately address students by name and follow up, if need be. People behave differently when they know you can call them by name instead of being an anonymous face in a crowd. Knowing your students by name also increases your comfort and confidence when you meet their parents for the first time at back-to-school events or respond to parent phone calls during the first weeks of school.

First minutes

Most schools require teachers to take attendance at the start of each class and report absences. Particularly important the first day of school is making sure that students are in the right class at the right time. For the new middle school student who is not accustomed to dealing with lockers and switching classrooms and teachers, the first couple days of school can be overwhelming, especially at a large school. Some students come into class late and start out stressed and worried. What happens in those first few minutes can make a huge difference in their attitudes about the teacher and the class.

Some teachers give students an assigned seat on the first day, but I prefer to say, "Sit wherever you would like for today. We will be doing a seating chart in a few days." You can learn a lot about your students in those few minutes as you watch the fascinating dynamics of students choosing seats. Who prefers to sit in the back? Who tries to save seats for their friends? Do any students self-advocate and ask to sit near the front to compensate for a vision or hearing limitation? Years of teaching middle school have taught me that the one consistent behavior is that the students will typically segregate by gender. It is not unusual for a student to comment, "Hey, all of the boys are on this side of the room, and all of the girls are on that side."

Strategy for assigning seats

If you do choose to assign seats, you might try making the arrangement by birthday order rather than alphabetical by last name. Tell them that they are in a particular order, and challenge them to ask each other questions to figure out what the order is. Usually someone guesses within a few minutes. Then ask for all of the January birthdays to raise their hands, then February, month by month through December. This can become a math activity, similar to "Names Count." Have students count the number of birthdays for each month and make a graph of the findings. Another activity is to have them figure what percentage of students were born in each month, in the first and second halves of the year, or in each of the four seasons.

Calling the roll

Once students are seated, it is time to call roll for the first time. I have learned that how a teacher goes about this simple task can make the difference between starting off on the right foot with a student and creating an obstacle that will be very difficult to overcome. Although a majority of students go by the first name that you see printed on your roster, some do not. Some students prefer a shortened version: Ben instead of Benjamin, Abby instead of Abigail, and so on. A few students go by their middle names, and students who attended their small elementary schools did not know their first names. Their teachers all knew not to call Tyler by his first name, which was Horace. If that bit of information does not get relayed to all of his new teachers, Tyler's first day of middle school may be a bad memory of students laughing about his name. So, how do you avoid embarrassing students and alienating them from the start? The script that I use goes something like this:

> Hello, everyone. Welcome to 5th period Spanish class. My name is Mrs. Stockton. The first thing that I need to do is take attendance to make sure that everyone is in the right class, because I know it can be a bit confusing the first day or two of school. (*Note: This can help minimize embarrassment if you do have a student who is in the wrong place.*) I have a list of names for this class, but before I read the list I would like to know if anyone goes by a first name that may be different from what is on the list. Some people prefer shorter versions of their names or go by their middle names. For example, my first name is Callyandra, but all of my friends and family call me Cally. If someone calls me on the phone and asks for "Callyandra," I know that they have gotten my name off of a list somewhere and are probably trying to sell me something. If you would like to let me know about a first name preference, please tell me your last name so that I can find it on the roster. Then you can tell me what you use for your first name so that I can make a note to help me remember. So, if I were a student in the class, I would raise my hand and tell the teacher that my last name is Stockton, and the first name I prefer is Cally. (*Note: Using this strategy, a student does not even have to say, "My name is Horace, but call me Tyler." He can say, "My last name is Johnson, and I go by Tyler."*)

Then I say, "Raise your hand if you need for me to make a change to your first name on the list." I have always had at least a few students raise their hands and tell me their name preferences. The changes are usually minor—Nick instead of Nicholas, Maddy instead of Madeline—but there are often looks of relief and appreciation on students' faces when they are given the opportunity to avoid being called by names that they do not prefer.

Difficult names to pronounce

After I make the requested changes, I take a moment to get help with names that may be difficult to pronounce. Here is part two of the script:

> Now that we have all of the first names recorded the way you want them, I need to ask if any of you have a first or last name that is hard for some people to pronounce or maybe isn't pronounced quite the way it looks. If you are worried that I may make a mess of it, please raise your hand and let me know what your name is so that I can make note of the correct way to say it. (*Note: Some students from other countries will choose to use an English pronunciation of their name to avoid being different, so don't insist on pronouncing the "g" in Sergio like an "h" if he says that he prefers it with a "j" sound. After you get to know him, you may want to have a conversation with him about what his family calls him, and whether he might actually prefer the pronunciation of his native language if he had some reassurance that his peers could learn to say it correctly.*)

Although this may look like a lot of preparation just to call the roll for the first time, it only takes a few minutes, and the rapport it establishes is well worth the time. As I read off all of the names and make eye contact when each student raises his or her hand, I say something positive such as "Pleased to meet you" or "Welcome to the class."

After taking attendance, I give the students a quick overview of the class and then play a name game so that I can begin to memorize their names, and the students can learn the names of classmates they do not know. I save the class rules and expectations for the next class period, because knowing who is in the class is my first priority. The "Name Snake" is the most efficient way for me to learn names, and students enjoy the physical activity of "Name Juggle," "Name Tarp Tag," and "Four Corners." The games in this section are a great way to start the school year and can be repeated if a new student joins the class.

Name Snake

Objective: To learn each other's names

Materials: Best done in a classroom, with desks in rows

Number of People: Best for 10–30

Time: About 30 seconds times the number of people (5–15 minutes)

Directions: This game is called "Name Snake" because you "snake" up and down the rows of desks, rather than starting at the front of each row. The first person says his or her name; the second person says the first person's name, then his or her own name; the third person says the first person's name, the second person's name, and then his or her own, until the last person says everyone's name and then his or her own.

Teacher Tip: To learn your students' names more quickly, look at each student as that person says his or her own name. As students say the names of their classmates, say each name to yourself. If a student gets stumped, be ready to help with a hint ("Starts with the letter J," or "It's the name of a famous ____.") Be careful not to use hints that might embarrass students. When the game is done, try to say all the names yourself.

Teaching Points:

Learning Strategy: Point out that repetition is a key factor in learning and memorizing. Students hear the name of the first student most often. With each additional student, they hear the name less often, and they hear the name of the person right before them only once. Students often stumble on that name, even though they have just heard it. To apply this to their studying, students should go through flashcards several times and shuffle them to see and say them in different orders.

Social/Cultural: Names are very important. Addressing someone by the name he or she wishes to be called is a sign of respect. Discuss using titles with names (Mr., Mrs., Miss, Ms., Dr., Rev., Captain, etc.) and waiting for permission to use first names with adults. Names can also be part of a family tradition. Ask how many students were named after a relative. (Social studies critical thinking question: Why do you think that in some cultures it has been more common for sons to be named after their fathers than for daughters to be named after their mothers?)

Variation:

A student hands an object (foam ball, "talking stick," or other item) to the next person after saying that next person's name. This version is particularly useful if you want to establish a classroom norm of "the person with the item is the one who gets to speak" during certain kinds of activities.

Modification: If you have a student with a memory or speech problem, seat her so that she can go first or second. You can also describe the activity, tell the students which side of the room is the starting point, and let a few students trade seats to experience more or less of a memory challenge. (Often, students will ask if they can try saying all of the names, even if they aren't the last person.)

Note: Remind students to practice good listening skills while other students take their turns saying the names.

Name Juggle

Objective: To learn each other's names and to practice working together

Materials: Foam ball or other soft object to throw, stopwatch or clock with second hand; can be done inside or outside

Number of People: Best for 10–30

Time: About 30 seconds times the number of people (5–15 minutes, more for variations)

Directions: Have the students stand in a circle, say a person's name, and toss the foam ball to that person. They cannot throw to the students next to them. The goal of the game is for each person to get the ball only one time and not leave anyone out. Do not let the students ask any questions or make any suggestions before the first round. Record how long it takes to do it the first time. Let the students share strategies (e.g., having people sit down once they get the ball); then set a time goal and repeat. This can be repeated a few times if the students want to reach a particular time goal. (A realistic minimum time is about one second per person.)

Teaching Points:

Observe the group dynamics. Who shows leadership? Who offers encouragement? Who hangs back? How does the group react if someone drops the ball?

Variations:

- For established groups: Talk with one student privately ahead of time and have him be the one to "drop the ball" or take a long time to throw to the next person so that you can observe and process the group's reaction. (Pick a student who is not necessarily a popular leader but someone who can handle some pressure from the group.) After you talk about the group reactions, let the group know that the student was a "plant" to create that group dynamic.

- The "juggling version": To increase complexity, add a second ball of a different color. Every person needs to have his or her name called twice and to get each ball. Then add a third ball.

Modification: If a student is unable to throw a ball, but can work the stopwatch, have that student be the timer.

Name Tarp Tag

Objective: To learn each other's names

Materials: A large plastic tarp, blanket, or dark sheet; best done outside or in a large space

Number of People: Best for 12–30

Time: 15–20 minutes

Directions: Divide the students into two groups. Have two volunteers hold each end of the tarp to make a wall between the two groups. (Lower the tarp while you are giving directions so that you can see everyone.) Have one group stand together on each side of the tarp wall so that the other side cannot see them when the tarp is raised.

Rules: A member from each team will come up to the tarp, at the count of three the tarp will be lowered quickly and the first person to correctly say the other person's name captures that person to their side. Everyone must go once before anyone repeats. If the names are said at the same time (ties), the two people trade places to join the other teams. Tarp holders are the judges. If more than one person on a team goes up at once when the tarp is lowered, the person on the other side gets to pick one to capture. If no one from a team is ready when the tarp is lowered, the person on the other team at the tarp gets to capture anyone from the opposing team. You can play until there are only two or three people left on one side, then redivide the groups and play again.

Tips for holding the tarp: It helps to hold one corner as high as possible (so students can't see over) and put a foot on the other corner to keep it on the ground. Rotate tarp holders after several rounds so that everyone gets to play.

Teaching Points:

Observe the group dynamics. (It's almost impossible to play this game without pointing.) After the game, ask students to rate their own participation with a show of hands—number of fingers up (0–5) for how well they participated.

Variation:

Divide into teams (boys vs. girls or mixed teams). Once someone is captured, they are out—held prisoner on the other side so it is possible to see who wins (the first team to capture all of the other team).

Notes: Remind students that this is not a contact sport. Some students will get very excited and start pushing others toward the tarp to take a turn. Other students will try to hide by crouching down or lying on the ground when the tarp is lowered. Establish rules for where and how to stand so that the player can be seen when the tarp is lowered.

Four Corners

Objective: To learn each other's names

Number of People: 12–30

Materials: Space to move and four corners

Time: 5 minutes per round

Directions: Do this activity after "Name Snake" or another quick activity in which all of the students have heard everyone's name. The teacher can be the "leader," or another student can run the game.

Pick a student to be the "center." The leader tells the center to cover her eyes and tells everyone else to "scramble" to a corner. After everyone is in a corner, the leader tells the center to pick someone. Without looking, the center says, "The corner with ____ (and names a student)." The center then uncovers her eyes and looks to see which corner that person is in. The center then needs to name the people who are with the target person. Those people are out and go sit down (the target person first named stays in). If the center does not remember the name of someone in the group, that person stays in and tells the center his name.

The center then covers her eyes again, and the second round starts (i.e., the leader says "scramble," everyone moves to a corner, and the center names another person). As the game advances and fewer students are left, take one or more corners out of play to limit the choices until almost everyone is out. Depending on the size of the group, do two rounds using all four corners, then two rounds using three corners, then two rounds using two corners.

If the target person named is the only one in that corner, then he or she is out. When only two people are left, have them do "rock, paper, scissors" or flip a coin to see which one wins. The winner becomes the center.

Keep the game moving quickly so that everyone can get back into the game soon. If students are slow to commit to a corner or keep trying to change, the leader can do a countdown: "You must be in a corner in 5, 4, 3, 2, 1."

Modification: If a student is not mobile, give him a whiteboard, marker, and eraser and have him mark the chosen corner and hold up the board. Put a landmark, such as a door, on the whiteboard so the orientation of the four corners is clear. Make sure the center looks at the board to see if the immobile student is included in the corner with the target person named.

Note: Some students may try to stand between two locations or change location after someone is named. Tell them they must commit. You can have them point to the corner to be clearer.

Name Association Games

Objective: To learn each other's names; to practice listening skills and phonemic awareness

Materials: None; students may use a dictionary or an atlas for some variations of the game sheet; best done outside or in a large space

Number of People: Best for 10–30

Time: 15–20 minutes

Directions for "My name is Zoe and I like zebras": Students introduce themselves individually, saying their names and something they like that starts with that same beginning letter and sound. For example, "My name is Annie and I like apples." (Note: George must like something with a soft "g," like giant giraffes, and not something with a hard "g," like grapes. Similarly, Carla can like cats, not chocolate.) After all students have introduced themselves, point to a student and ask another student to say his or her name and what he or she likes. Repeat with several students and see how well they listened and remembered.

Directions for "My name is Alan and I'm from Argentina": This is similar to the "I like" game, above, but the place each student comes from must start with the same beginning sound and letter as the name. The leader can specify that it must be a country, state, or city, or it can be anything that makes sense. "I am Cathy, and I'm from Canada (or California, or Columbus, or the countryside). After all students have introduced themselves, point to a student and ask someone else to say his or her name and where he or she is from. Repeat with several students to see how well they listened and remembered.

Variations:

- First person says "My name is ____ and I like (or am from) ____." Second person says what the first person's name is and what he or she likes and then says, "My name is ____, and I like ____." Third person tells the second person's name or like and his or her own. (Each person only records the previous person's and his or her own name and like.)

- Long variation (recommended for small groups only): Like "Name Snake," each person says each person's name since the start, what that person likes or where he or she comes from, and then adds his or her own.

- Use particular categories for the word association (food, animals, book authors, or musicians.)

Note: Set ground rules for respect and allow no inappropriate comments or associations with anyone's name.

Heads Up, Seven Up

Objective: To learn each other's names; to work on participation, taking turns to include everyone in the activity

Materials: None; best done with students sitting at desks/tables

Number of People: Best for 14–30, but can be done with fewer (see Variations below)

Time: About 5 minutes per round. Good filler activity to settle students down when there are a few minutes left.

Directions: Do this activity after "Name Snake" or another quick activity in which all of the students have heard everyone's name. The teacher can lead this activity or pick a student to be the leader.

The leader picks seven students to be up; they come to the front of the room. Then the leader says, "Heads down, thumbs up." The other students put their heads down on their desks and hold a thumb up. The seven students quietly walk around and tap the thumb of a student, who then puts his thumb down. After all seven students have tapped someone, they come back to the front of the room and stand in a line. The leader says, "Heads up, seven up." The students who were tapped stand up and the leader points to them one by one to guess who picked them. They need to say the student's name (not "you"). If they are correct, they take that person's place and become one of the seven up. If they are wrong, they sit back down. After everyone has guessed, the leader tells those who are still up front to point to and say the name of the student they picked. This activity can be repeated for several rounds. Set a goal for all students to be picked at least once.

Variations:

- To play with a smaller group, have fewer students up, and when the students guess, have each person respond "maybe" and then reveal who they picked all at once, after everyone has guessed. With small groups, it is a good idea to have half of the students up so that everyone gets picked. If there is an odd number, have one be the leader.

- To play with a larger group, more than seven people can be up.

- Let students take turns being the leader. Have the leader start from different sides of the room each time to have students guess.

NOTES: If a student hits or twists thumbs instead of "tapping," make her sit out. You can let her back in the game after a round or two if she agrees to behave appropriately.

Sometimes students will conspire and say, "Everyone guess Billy." Watch to see if you need to intervene or just let that strategy play itself out.

Students may accuse others of peeking. Just remind the students that if it looks like they are peeking, they probably won't get picked.

Names Count

Objective: Have fun learning each other's names and practice math

Materials: Paper and pens/pencils; whiteboard, chalkboard, or flipchart paper

Number of People: 10 or more

Time: 10–20 minutes

Directions: Look at your roster; find the first name with the fewest letters and the one with the most letters. Have the students take out a piece of paper and draw a grid with enough boxes to cover all of the possibilities between the fewest and most and label the boxes. For example, if you have a Ty and a Zachariah, you need boxes for 2 letters, 3 letters…up to 9 letters.

2 Letters	3 Letters	4 Letters
Ed	Bob Ann Tom Joe	Jill Sean
5 Letters	**6 Letters**	**7 Letters**
Julie Frank	Jessie Taylor	Jessica William Abigail
8 Letters	**9 Letters**	**10 Letters**
Brittany Harrison	Jefferson	Alexandria

Tell the students to put their own names in the box with the matching number of letters. Have the students go around to each of their classmates, introduce themselves, and add each name to the box that has that number of letters. When they are done, have them count the names to make sure they have as many as are on the roster.

Tell the students to count the number of names in each box and write that number somewhere in the box. Create a list on the board of the tally for each box (2 letter names = 1, 3 letter names = 4, etc.).

Teaching Points:

What is the mode? (most frequent) What is the median? (average)

What percent/fraction of the total names has 3 (etc.) letters?

Create a graph and/or pie chart of the data.

If this list is representative of the population of students in their grade, what is the probability that a new student joining the class would have 4 (etc.) letters in his or her first name?

Variation:

Use last names in the activity if you want students to learn them.

Play My Name

Objective: To have fun learning each other's full names

Materials: Handout (master attached) and musical instrument (xylophone, recorder, keyboard)

Number of People: 5–30

Time: 10–15 minutes to create melody, (depending on students' understanding of musical staff), plus 15 minutes to write lyrics (sharing time depends on number of students)

Directions: Give the students a handout of the key and have them figure out what note goes with each letter of the alphabet. Have them write their first and last name using the notes and put the notes on the music staff. Then have them play the notes to see what it sounds like.

More advanced: Have them experiment using quarter notes, half notes, and whole notes to create a rhythm and melody that they like.

Even more advanced: Have them write a short jingle about themselves to go with the melody, using one word (or one syllable) for each note. (For Bob Smith: "I am Bob. I am tall and smart.")

Options for introducing/sharing:

   a. Students play their melodies for the class: "This is what Abraham Lincoln sounds like…"

   b. Students share their melodies in pairs or small groups.

Teaching Points:

Musical staff, quarter, half, and whole notes

Variation:

Have a contest for the best melody or jingle. Decide if you want to have judges (top music students?) or student vote (open or secret ballot).

Key of Alphabet Letters to Music Notes

A	B	C	D	E	F	G
A	B	C	D	E	F	G
H	I	J	K	L	M	N
O	P	Q	R	S	T	U
V	W	X	Y	Z	Ñ	

Example of writing a first and last name and filling in corresponding musical note below the letter:

A	b	r	a	h	a	m	L	i	n	c	o	l	n							
A	B	D	A	A	A	F	E	B	G	C	A	E	G							

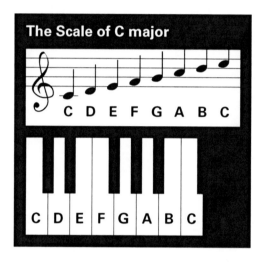

Example of putting the "name notes' on the musical staff:

A b r a h a m L i n c o l n

Write your first and last names and fill in the corresponding musical note below the letter.

Write your "name notes" notes on the musical staff. Add words to create a short song.

Getting Better Acquainted

An important part of building a positive learning environment is finding ways for students to get to know each other so they can find out what they have in common and learn to respect their differences. Middle school students need opportunities and encouragement to meet a variety of classmates, especially students who attended different elementary schools. One way to prevent or break cliques and to discourage bullying is to model respect for each student as an individual. Setting the tone at the beginning of the school year and continuing to help students get to know each other as the year progresses is important.

Knowing more about the students' backgrounds and interests also helps the teacher find connections and motivators within the curriculum. A teacher can introduce a reluctant reader to a book that relates to his or her favorite activity or give a student with a particular hobby examples showing how certain math skills are crucial to that hobby. Students also appreciate knowing a few things about their teachers so that they can relate to them as real people.

Many middle school students love to talk about themselves, their families, their pets—anything you would like to know and a few things you probably don't need to know. (One of the delicate jobs of a teacher is anticipating when a student's story needs to be intercepted and redirected.) Other students are shy and don't reveal much about themselves. The goal of the activities in this section is to give everyone an opportunity to share some information in a fun way. They are fast-paced so that shy students do not feel "on the spot" for too long, and more verbose students will not dominate.

Show and Tell activities

In keeping with the active and interactive nature of this book, I did not include lesson plans for the more presentational type of "show and tell" activity, but I will mention a few here. These activities can be more interactive if you allow for a short question-and-answer time after each presentation.

- "Me Poster" or "Me Collage": Students make a poster that describes themselves and share the poster in small groups or in front of the class. You can leave the assignment open-ended, or you can ask students to be sure to include certain things—something you are good at, your favorite place, and so on.

- "Me Bag" or "Me Box": Ask students to bring in a certain number of objects that represent their lives. The objects need to fit in a grocery sack or shoe box. Students take turns showing the items and explaining what each one represents.

- Higher Tech Versions: If you have access to a computer lab, have students create a slide show (PowerPoint) about themselves to share with the class.

- "Shout-outs": Give students opportunities to share what they did over the weekend, any good news, and so on. Shout-outs can be open-ended (anything they want to share), or you can have students respond to a particular question (as simple as "What is your favorite thing to eat for breakfast?"). Be mindful of cultural differences. For example, not everyone celebrates the same holidays, so "What was your best Christmas gift?" may leave some students out.

Formative Assessment

Some of the activities in this section are flexible enough that you can adapt them for checking on students' progress in the content areas. For example, the Paired Venn Diagram is a useful tool for checking students' ability to compare. Most middle school students compare plant and animal cells in their life science classes. One student of the pair can be responsible for the plant characteristics; the other student details the animal characteristics; their goal, like that in the activity as presented in this section, is to find the cell characteristics that overlap, much like they did with each other's characteristics. The more times they construct a Venn diagram, the more practice they have in gaining analytical skills.

Another example of how to adapt an activity in this section for assessment purposes, is to use the People Bingo for a content review—matching plants with their seed, leaf, and flower forms or matching minerals, rocks, or planets with their distinguishing characteristics. Students with different ability levels can work on Bingo cards of appropriate complexity for their levels. If students create the Bingo cards, they review the material yet one more time.

Two Truths and a Lie

Objective: To learn more about each other; can be repeated whenever a new member joins the group or just for fun

Materials: 3 slips of paper per person, pens/pencils

Number of People: Best for 10–30

Time: 5 minutes to think and write, and 1–2 minutes per person to share (can be done in more than one session)

Directions: First model the activity by sharing three things about you and asking the students to guess which one is not true. Then, have the students write down three things about themselves on three separate slips of paper: two things that are true and one thing that is not true but might fool everyone. Three slips of paper work better here than one; students can shuffle them before speaking and not have to decide if the lie should be first, second, or third.

Give the students some suggestions: places they've been, unusual things about their families or pets, famous relatives, hobbies, and so on. Give the students five minutes to think and write. Students then take turns coming to the front of the class to read their three items. (This is good practice for later public speaking.) They then call on two class members to guess which one is the lie. (They usually call on students who do not know them well to prevent their best friends from easily making a correct guess.) If two people guess wrong, the student whose turn it was has stumped the audience and can write his or her name on the board under "Best Bluffer." The bluffer picks a student to go next.

If you need to use two sessions for the activity, have the remaining students put their names or initials on their slips of paper and give them to you to hold until next time.

Variations:

- Allow some time for follow-up questions and discussion. Because students come up with some very interesting facts about themselves, other students may want to share their similar interests and experiences.

- Take notes about each student and give them all a quiz the next time you meet to see how well they listened and remembered the facts. (Examples: Whose uncle was an NFL quarterback? How many broken bones has Bob had in his life? How many pets does Sue have?)

Note: A few students tend to usually volunteer to guess which one is the lie. You may want to set an expectation that each student can only guess a certain number of times or have another strategy in mind to make sure that everyone participates during the guessing.

Paired Venn Diagram

Objective: To learn more about each other; can be repeated whenever a new member joins the group or just for fun

Materials: paper and pens/pencils

Number of People: 2 or more, students working in pairs

Time: 10 minutes to think and write, and 2 minutes per pair to share (can be done in more than one session)

Directions: Explain the activity and give an example on the board so that students understand how to use the Venn diagram before you pair them.

Pair the students by drawing names or passing out cards and have students find their partner. Have the students ask each other questions until they come up with five things they have in common (Examples: have brown hair, play soccer, have brothers) and five things each that are not true for the other person (Examples: has a cat/has a dog, likes country music/likes rock). You can make it more challenging by ruling out the obvious common connections (the same grade, the same age).

Have the students complete a Venn diagram by putting the things they have in common in the area of the overlapping circles and what is different about each of them in their respective sides of the circle.

Have the students share their Venn diagrams with the rest of the class or post the diagrams for students to read on their own.

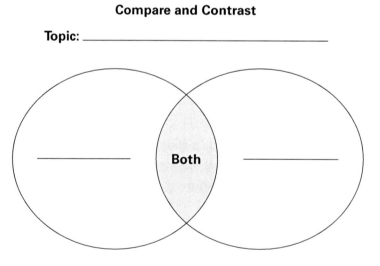

Compare and Contrast

Topic: _____

Both

Variation:

Have students complete a separate Venn diagram with two or three other students. Depending on the amount of time you have, you can increase or decrease the number of similarities and differences for them to list.

Human Shuffle

Objective: To interact with classmates to discover commonalities and differences; good intro for peer pressure discussions

Number of People: Best for 8–20

Time: 10–20 minutes (depending on number of rounds and amount of discussion)

Materials: Some space to spread out, a seat for each student or a carpet square to stand on

Directions: This activity is a bit like musical chairs. Put the chairs in a circle, one chair for each student. The leader stands in the center and does not have a chair. The leader makes a statement ("Shuffle if you like chocolate"). If the statement is true for a student, he or she gets up and moves to a vacated seat. The leader tries to take a vacated seat as well, so one student will be left without a seat and becomes the new leader. (If the leader doesn't get to a seat quickly enough, he will need to make another statement.) The new leader makes another "Shuffle if you…" statement.

Statements can be preferences (likes, dislikes), birth month, what students are wearing, experiences. See "People Bingo" and "Vote with Your Feet" for more ideas.

You can stop and debrief when there are surprises and notable responses (no one moves, everyone moves).

Variations:

- Limit the questions to a particular topic.
- Instead of chairs, have students stand on carpet squares or other placeholders.
- Questions can elicit opinions that quickly can lead to a debate. For example: "Shuffle if you think school uniforms are a good idea." After they move, ask, "For those of you who moved, why do you think so?" "For those who didn't move, why not?"

Modification: Students with disabilities who are not able to quickly move to new spots can point to a new spot with a laser pointer, flashlight, or yardstick, and that spot is theirs.

Note: In musical chairs-type activities, some students can get rowdy and fight for a spot. Establish ground rules ahead of time.

People Bingo

Objective: To learn more about each other

Materials: Bingo forms and pens/pencils; if you repeat the activity with the same group, add new items to the bingo card

Number of People: Best for 10–30

Time: 15–20 minutes

Directions: Create a bingo template with characteristics about people (e.g., only child, moved more than once, three or more pets) and have students walk around the room and ask each other the questions. If they find a match, they ask the person to write his or her first name in the appropriate box. They can only sign one square per student, unless it is a small group, and they need to sign more than one square to meet the goal. Set a limit—one, two, or three signatures from the same person—so that students don't stay with one or two people to fill the whole card.

The first person to get names in all 25 boxes (or 20 of the 25 boxes, depending on the size of the group and how many bingo boxes you want filled) wins. Give a small prize if you wish. Keep playing until everyone has the needed number of names.

After everyone has filled the boxes, ask students to read an item and the name of the person who was a match. Try to include items from the "multiple intelligences" on the bingo card so that you have a good variety.

Variations:

- Change items on the sample bingo form. Ask students for suggestions.
- Instead of filling 20 or 25 boxes, you can create a few different versions of the form (i.e., scramble the items); the first person to get five in a row (vertical, horizontal, or diagonal) wins.

Notes: How do you know if someone faked an answer to fill a box? You don't. You can't check out all the facts, so you have to rely on the students' honesty. Some students may call out others for cheating ("Joe isn't an only child. I know his sister!").

People Bingo

Find someone who matches each description below. That person writes his or her name in the appropriate box. You may only get _____ box(es) signed by each person.

Was born in a different state.	Is an only child.	Has more than three pets.	Is left-handed.	Loves to read.
Can play a musical instrument.	Plays two or more sports.	Has never had a broken bone or stitches.	Has visited a country outside the U.S.	Does not like ice cream.
Was named after a relative.	Likes to ski or snowboard.	Can draw really well.	Knows at least a dozen words in another language.	Likes to cook.
Likes to build things.	Is a whiz at mathematics.	Belongs to a club or organization.	Has a "green thumb." (Has a garden/ lots of plants).	Collects something. (stamps, coins, etc.).
Has memorized a poem (and can still recite it).	Has very neat handwriting.	Likes to go hiking, fishing, or hunting.	Has volunteered or donated to a charity.	Likes to shop.

Vote With Your Feet

Objective: To interact with classmates to discover commonalities and differences; a good intro for peer pressure discussions

Materials: Space to spread out

Number of People: Any number, but best for 10 or more

Time: : 15–20 minutes (depending on number of rounds and amount of discussion)

Directions: Tell students they will be sharing their opinions about a variety of topics by standing along a continuum. They are to think about the choices offered and move to the side of the room that best matches their preference. If they have a very strong preference, they go toward the end of the line. If they don't have any preference, they stand in the middle. Establish ground rules: No put-downs allowed. Students sit out a round if they make a negative comment. Students shouldn't try to persuade others, verbally or nonverbally, to join their side.

Start with some easy questions that are relevant to the age group. For example: "Do you prefer soccer or football?" (If you prefer soccer, move to this side. If you prefer football, move to that side. If you don't like either or like them both the same, stand in the middle.) Ask someone from the extreme soccer side to respond to "Why do you like soccer?" Ask someone from the extreme football side to respond to "Why do you like football?" Ask a couple people why they are in the middle.

Here are some other example questions: Country music or rock 'n' roll? Best pets—dogs or cats? Pizza or ice cream? Playing video games or watching a movie? Summertime or winter ? Skateboarding or snowboarding? Snowboarding or skiing? Italian food or Mexican food (or Chinese, Indian, Thai…)? Reading a book or listening to music? Have the students come up with some questions.

Debriefing: Get some comments regarding what they've learned. Any surprises with what they had in common? Students can also write a short reflection.

Variations:

Use this activity to start a debate of more complex topics. After students have picked a side, have them argue their position and see if they can persuade anyone to move to their side.

Math Variation:

Do percentages/fractions of students that hold certain positions. Or, have the students pick a classmate and calculate what percentage of the time they agreed with each other.

Modification: Give students with limited mobility whiteboards to mark their preferences (or rulers to point out the direction and amount of preference) and be sure to include their responses.

Backward Name "Ym Eman Si"

Objective: Students describe themselves using opposite qualities to learn something about each other

Number of People: 5–30

Time: Varies

Materials: Name tags or table tents, markers, chalkboard or whiteboard if shared in front of class

Directions: Give the students a name tag or table tent and have them write their first name backward. (If you have any palindromes—such as Bob, Hannah, or Anna—have them use their middle names or last names.) Then have students write three descriptions of themselves that are the opposite of their true nature. For example, if Mia loves sports, she could write "I hate sports." If Brian is very talkative, he could write "I am very shy." Give the class a few minutes to think and write.

Options for Introducing/Sharing:

a. Students write their backward name on the board, pronounce it for the class, and give their three opposite descriptions. (Have them try to do it with a straight face.)

b. Students get in pairs, introduce themselves to each other, and take turns introducing their partners to the group: "This is Ydoc. He hates football, is quiet, and always keeps his room clean."

c. *Medium Risk Option:* Students ask three other people, individually, what they think would be a good opposite description and write down their suggestions.

d. *Higher Risk Option:* Students write their backward name on the board and let volunteers from the class offer descriptions they think would be opposite.

Discussion: Ask students what they learned about their classmates by hearing what they think are their opposite qualities. If you used the variation letting class volunteers offer descriptions, what did the students learn about themselves based on their classmates' descriptions?

Teaching Points:

Synonyms, antonyms, palindromes

Variation:

Expand the opposite counterpart scenario by having the class figure out where the opposite place on earth would be that they are all from. (Opposite in terms of longitude and latitude? Opposite in terms of geography, elevation, climate?) Or, figure out where the opposite place in space would be. (Most opposite planet?)

Note: Look over the roster and make sure that there are no embarrassing or profane-sounding backward names.

Warm-Ups and Attention-Getters

Most middle school students are social, curious, and highly distractible. It is hard for a teacher to compete with the glittery fingernail polish of the girl in the third row, the boy that can turn his eyelids inside out, the cool sound that you can make with a piece of paper and the little plastic comb they give everyone on picture day—not to mention the host of other visual, auditory, tactile, and olfactory stimuli in the classroom. Getting and keeping everyone's attention is challenging. The expression "herding cats" comes to mind.

As students move from classroom to classroom and subject to subject, they need to refocus and get prepared for each teacher's "plan for the day." Most teachers teach (prep) between one and four different classes, and, depending on their school, students often have between six and nine different classes. They move from math to phys ed to English to art to geography; at the start of each class they must jump back in where the class ended the last time. (Even more challenging is for my beginning Spanish students to switch languages when they come to class!)

Teachers know that students' attention is influenced by the time of day, weather, day of the week, upcoming or recent holidays (especially those that involve sugar), and a variety of other environmental and bio-chemical influences, not to mention the myriad individual circumstances on students' minds. Students' constant use of high-speed Internet, instant messaging, and other on-demand communications and entertainment, as well as the frenetic pace of videogames lead many parents and teachers to think students' attention spans are getting shorter. Whether or not there has been a decrease in the length of time that a student can focus, the fact remains that teachers need strategies for getting students' attention, and they have to be more effective and creative than repeating the rhetorical question, "Can I have your attention, please?"

Middle school students need some routine and predictability in their days. They also need variety and some unexpected stimulation to capture their attention. We all have experienced how the motivational or educational poster on the wall soon becomes invisible because we become so used to it being there. Moving it to a different location or even just hanging it at a new angle suddenly makes it visible again.

I love to keep my students on their toes, and I'm sure they think I'm a bit "loca" (but in a good way, or so they say). Use humor and puns, and play on words. ("Please put your hand down until I finish the directions, or I will lose my train of thought, and then I'll have to take the bus.") Bring in props to add visual interest to the poem, story problem, or historical event that you are studying. I predict that an old tire showing up in the middle of your classroom will generate more interest and excitement than a full-color slide presentation.

Enhancing creativity. Many of the activities in this section have the capacity to foster creativity in students; once students get the "hang" of the games, let THEM take the games in new directions. For example, "If You Can Hear Me" offers students the opportunity to come up with a visual language— show me latitude, show me longitude, show me friction—what other concepts can they portray? What other methods can they use to communicate/represent the concepts? "Finish the Phrase" allows for students to think of alternate endings for common expressions, and "Amazing Math" has them approach math from a different perspective than usual—hopefully with a new understanding or at least wonderment for the beauty of math.

Note: This introduction and the following activities are based on my experience with typical middle school students. When it comes to meeting the needs of students who are diagnosed with an attention deficit disorder, I rely on the recommendations of specialists to modify their learning environments and activities

If You Can Hear Me...

Objective: Get students' attention, classroom management for transitions

Materials: None

Number of People: Any number

Time: 1 minute or less

Directions: I have heard some teachers use the technique "If you can hear me, clap once. If you can hear me, clap twice." The students who didn't hear you the first time hear the other students clap and then are supposed to stop talking and join in on the double clap. This usually works pretty well, although I have seen a few chatty students continue to talk to their neighbors while they are clapping twice.

I have taken this strategy and added a twist that my students enjoy. "If you can hear me, clap once. If you can hear me, clap twice. If you can hear me, clap five times." Then, when they clap five times, I take a deep bow and say, "Thank you. Thank you very much."

I also like to use surprise options other than clapping. "If you can hear me, touch your nose." "If you can hear me, close your eyes." "If you can hear me, pat your head and rub your stomach."

Some world language teachers use a technique called TPR (total physical response), in which words are associated with a particular motion. "If you can hear me, show me 'cocinar'" (stirring motion like they are cooking). "If you can hear me, show me 'tocar la guitarra'" (guitar strumming motion).

Some music teachers have hand motions for do-re-me-fa-so-la-te-do and could get a choir's attention with, "If you can hear me, show me 'la.'"

Here are a few ideas. Can you think of others for your content area?

Math: "If you can hear me, show me a right angle." "...show me parallel." "...show me less than." "...show me greater than." "...show me perpendicular."

Geography: "If you can hear me, show me latitude." "...show me longitude."

Science: "If you can hear me, show me friction." (rub hands together)

Notes: Seasoned teachers will tell you that it is more effective to say "If you can hear me..." in a normal or even quieter voice. Trying to talk over the students defeats the purpose. Be ready to move on with the next activity as soon as they have stopped talking and have done the requested number of claps or the motion.

Finish the Phrase

Objective: Get students' attention; talk about "cultural literacy" and common expressions

Materials: List of phrases; paper and pencil for written variation

Number of People: Any number

Time: 2–20 minutes, depending on number of phrases shared and variation used

Directions: Say the first part of a phrase and then pause. Students say the words that complete the phrase. For example:

I pledge allegiance (to the flag)	What goes up (must come down)	Four score (and seven years ago)
I'm a little teapot, (short and stout)	The itsy, bitsy (spider)	Here comes (the bride) or (the judge)
Once upon (a time)	Happy birthday (to you)	Play (ball)

Variations:

Instead of calling out the answers, students write them to see how many they can get right.

- Students suggest famous quotes or expressions to finish.

- Students come up with alternative endings to some expressions. Examples: You can lead a horse to water, but _____ . Between a rock and _____ . A penny saved is _____ . Out of the frying pan and _____ .

- This activity is also a great classroom management tool. Rather than saying "Please be quiet," make a habit of throwing in a pair of "Finish the Phrase" prompts and students will get quiet so that they can hear the clue.

- Reinforce a school motto (Failure is… not an option!) or a key concept (Don't forget to… conjugate your verbs)!

Notes: Some students will want to go on and say the whole expression or rhyme, or sing the whole song, so either be prepared to listen to all of "I'm a little teapot" or be ready to move on with the next item.

Basta

Objective: Get students' attention; review vocabulary, terminology, etc.

Materials: Paper and pencil; stack of letters; whiteboard, chalkboard, or overhead transparency

Number of People: Any number

Time: 15–20 minutes

Directions: : "Basta" is a Spanish word meaning "enough." This game can be created quickly and used for many different subjects. You can either create the score cards yourself and make copies to distribute, or you can have students make their own using a piece of paper.

The score cards have a row across the top with the categories (see example below). The far left column is for the letter of the alphabet that will be used, and the column on the right is for the score for each round. The blanks of the table are for each round of the game.

If the students are filling in the categories, write them on the board for them to copy. When everyone has their cards ready, start shuffling through the stack of letters and tell a student to say "basta" when he or she wants you to stop. When the student says "basta," write down the letter, and say it out loud. Now the students must come up with a word that starts with that letter for each of the categories. The first person to write a word in all of the columns shouts "basta," and everyone must stop writing. (They can finish the word they were writing if they had started it before the person said "basta.")

Ask the first student what word he or she has for each category. If no one else has that word, he or she gets two points for the word. If someone else has that word, everyone with that answer gets one point. Have everyone share their answers. Any unique answers (that are correct responses to the category) are worth 2 points. Any answers that match another student's choice are worth one point. Any items left blank are 0 points. Have the students put their score for that round at the end of that row. (In the example below, most of the items would be worth 1 point in a large class, because another student would probably think of the same one. "Paltry" would probably be worth two points.)

Letter	First/Last Name	Place	Food/Drink	Description (Adjective)	Action	Points
W	Washington 1	Wyoming 1	watermelon 1	worried 1	walking 1	5
P	Paul 1	Pittsburg 1	pie 1	paltry 2	------ 0	5

Go through the stack of letters again. Do as many rounds as time allows, with different students saying "basta." At the end, have the students add up their points. The highest score wins.

Variations:

- Depending on your categories, you can decide to leave some letters out of the stack (e.g., Q U, V, X, Z).
- Content category examples (Science: elements, parts of cell, planets, etc.)

AlphaBattle

Objective: Get students' attention and expand vocabulary

Materials: Piece of paper and pencil to keep score (optional: a large dictionary to challenge words)

Number of People: Any number

Time: 10–20 minutes

Directions: Divide students into pairs. (If there is an odd number, one student can be the keeper of the dictionary to look up challenged words.) Decide which student will go first. When the leader says "go," the first student says a word that starts with "A." The other student says a different word that starts with "A." Students must say a word within three seconds. They go back and forth until one of the students cannot come up with a word within three seconds or says a word that does not start with that letter ("phone" for letter "F"). When a student doesn't come up with a correct word in the three seconds, the other student gets a point and starts the next round with the next letter in the alphabet.

Play for a set amount of time. Use the rules from the game "Scrabble" (e.g., no proper nouns—and no profanity). The student with the most points at the end of the activity wins.

Optional Rule: If a student challenges the spelling or existence of a word, the leader looks it up. If it is not in the dictionary, the challenger gets two points. If it is in the dictionary, the student who was challenged gets two points. Once a challenged word has been decided, move on to the next letter of the alphabet.

Teaching Points:

What are some advantages of having an extensive vocabulary? What kinds of jobs would require you to know and use a lot of words?

Variations:

- Rather than starting with "A" (especially if you play this game more than once), start with another letter of the alphabet. If students get all the way to "Z," they can go back to "A."

- Instead of allowing any word from the dictionary, limit the category to a content area, such as a math-related word, a science word, a geography term or history word. (This becomes a paired, aloud version of "Basta.") If the category is very limited (like elements or countries), students may get completely stumped on some letters, and they will move through the alphabet more quickly. Part of the score will depend on luck—if they had to be the one to start the "V" or "X" list of words.

Amazing Math

Objective: Get students' attention and have them think creatively about math

Materials: Chalkboard or whiteboard, your hands

Number of People: Any number

Time: 15–20 minutes, depending on number of math facts or demonstrations you share

Directions:

Nifty Nines: Ask students how to tell if a number is divisible by nine. If you add the digits together, and the sum is nine, then the number is divisible by nine.

$36 = 3 + 6 = 9.$ $54 = 5 + 4 = 9.$
$6552 = 6 + 5 + 5 + 2 = 18 = 1 + 8 = 9.$

Hand calculator: You can also use your hands as a calculator when multiplying by nine. Hold all 10 fingers up in front of you. If you want to multiply four times nine, drop your fourth finger and count what is left on both sides—three fingers to the left and six fingers to the right. The answer is 36. What is 9 x 7? Drop the seventh finger—six to the left and three to the right = 63.

Square Five: You can square any two-digit number that ends in five (15, 25, 35, 45, 55, 65, 75, 85, 95) in two steps.

Step 1: Multiply the first digit by that same number, plus one.
Step 2: Put 25 on the end.

For example, to square 65,
Step 1: 6 x (6+1), which is 6 x 7 = 42
Step 2: put 25 on the end, and you get 4,225 (i.e., 65 x 65=4,225).

Double Digits Times Eleven: To multiply double-digit numbers by 11, split the digits of the number and put the sum of the digits in the middle. That number is the answer. For example, 24 x 11: split up the 2 and 4, add them together, put the sum (6) in the middle, and the answer is 264.

Guess Someone's Age: Ask someone to multiply the first number of his or her age by five. Add three. Double the figure. Tell the person to add the second number of his or her age to the figure and say the answer. Subtract six and you will have the person's age.

Repeating Age: Multiply your age by seven. Multiply that product by 1,443. Your age shows up over and over in the answer. For example: Sarah's age is 13.

$13 x 7 = 91$
$91 x 1,443 = 131,313$

Chisanbop: Chisanbop or chisenbop [from Korean chi (ji) finger + sanpŏp (sanbeop) calculation]is an abacus-like finger counting method used to perform basic mathematical operations. Chisanbop was created in the 1940s in Korea by Sung Jin Pai and revised by his son Hang Young Pai. It was brought to the U.S. around 1977 by Hang Young Pai. With this method, it is possible to display all numbers from zero to 99 with both hands. There are some examples on the Internet of how to use Chisanbop for simple calculations. Give it a try and then teach your students.

Memory Test

Objective: Get students' attention; have them think about ways to improve memory

Materials: Two deep boxes with lids, 12 items per box, paper and pencils

Number of People: Any number

Time: 15–20 minutes

Directions: Before class, get two deep boxes (the kind that reams of paper are packed in) and put 12 items in each box. In one box, make the items completely random—a key, a marble, a spoon, a pair of scissors, an apple. In the other box, put 12 related items—all things from the kitchen (spoon, fork, knife, measuring cup, small plate, sponge) or all office supplies (pencil, pen, scissors, tape) OR two groups of six related things (six kitchen things and six office things).

At the start of the activity, tell the students to number their papers from 1 to 12. Tell them you are going to show them a box of 12 items, and when you say "go," they are to write down as many things as they can remember from the box. You are going to show them row by row, and when everyone has looked in the box, you are going to tell the first row to start writing, then you are going to tell the second row to start writing, then the third, and so on. That way each row will have about the same amount of time to think and remember before they start writing. They are not to talk.

Start with the random box first. Walk down each row with it and have each student stand and look in the box for a few seconds. (Hold the box so that other students can't see inside ahead of time or after it has passed.) After you have made it around the room, tell the first row to start writing. Pause the length of time it took you to walk down a row and tell the second row to start writing. Pause again and then have the third row start, until everyone is writing. Give the students a few minutes to write what they could remember. Ask whether anyone remembered all twelve. See who had 9, 10, 11. Check to see how many of their listed items were correct.

Repeat the same process with the second box, starting from the other side of the room. Ask how many items they were able to remember the second time. Was it easier?

Teaching Points:

It is easier to remember things that are grouped together; categorizing focuses the brain to remember. Ask for some ways this can be applied to studying. If items are connected in some way, it helps. You could show the first box again and have the students make up a story about a few of the items. (A girl got out a key to go back into the house to find the spoon so that should could carry a marble …)

Anagrams

Objective: Get students' attention and practice thinking creatively

Materials: Paper and pencil, whiteboard, chalkboard or flipchart

Number of People: Any number

Time: 10–20 minutes

Directions: Model the activity first by writing a word on the board or flipchart, writing a few words that can be made from its letters, and then asking the students for a few more. Tell the students that you are going to give them a word, and they are to write that word at the top of the page; when you say "go," they need to come up with as many words as they can think of in X minutes, using the letters from that word.

Give the students a word that is at least six letters long (like "pirates"), and say "go." At the end of the time limit (three minutes or five minutes), say "Stop," and have everyone put their pencils down. Have the students count the number of words they created (pirates: trip, tea, tires, tries, pit …). You can have the winner say his or her words aloud, or you can collect the papers to check for spelling and the highest number of words.

Rules: Decide if plural words (rate and rates) count as two separate words. Decide if proper names count. (You may want to leave them out, since there can be many different spellings of names.)

Variations:

- You can do more than one round with a different starter word and have the score (word count) start over or be cumulative.

- Students can work together in pairs or small groups to brainstorm the list of words. There also can be a competition between groups.

- More Challenging Anagrams: Give a title or first and last name and have students come up with a phrase using the letters. Letters can only be used as often as they appear in the title/name. Example: "George Washington" has two "Es" and two "Os" and one "A" and one "I," so "E" and "O" can only be used twice in a phrase (e.g., "Engage rowing host"). Winners can be selected based on the best phrase or the most number of letters used in the phrase.

- Most Challenging Anagrams: Students must come up with a phrase that uses all of the letters. There are free anagram generators on the Internet that you can use to show students some of the many possibilities from each word or phrase, but encourage students to see how many they can create on their own.

Mental Vacation

Objective: Practice concentration, manage stress

Materials: None

Number of People: Any number

Time: 5–10 minutes

Directions: Before you start the activity, tell the students that they are going to use their powers of concentration to take a mini-vacation for the next five (or ten) minutes. Tell them that you will give them directions and ask them questions to help them create the vacation spot in their minds. (Use a normal, calm, and steady voice and pause between questions to give students time to think.)

Have students sit as comfortably as possible (not easy to do in most school desks) and close their eyes. Tell the students to begin by noticing what they hear and feel around them in the classroom—the clock ticking, the hum of the computer fan, the feel of the desk and chair, and so on. Tell them they now get to take a mini-vacation from school, and they get to choose the destination. Ask them to think of their ideal vacation spot.

Is it in this state or a different state? In a different country? Is it a beach? In the mountains? A theme park? Think of the place you would most like to be. It may be a favorite place you have visited before or a place that you haven't been to before now. What is the weather like? How does the temperature feel? What are you wearing? What sounds do you hear in this place? Who is with you on this vacation or are you enjoying the time alone? What are you doing right now? Are there any particular smells—water, foods, trees? What else do you notice about this place?

Take a moment to enjoy all of the sights, sounds, smells, and feelings. It's about time to come back to school, so take a final look around and remember that you can come back again when you need a mini-vacation to refresh your mind or when you are feeling frustrated or stressed. It doesn't cost anything, and you can create the scene that is perfect for you. As you leave your vacation spot and gradually come back to school, notice the sounds and feel of the classroom again. Open your eyes, and you'll see that you are back in room #_____.

Ask how many students were able to picture their vacation spots. Would anyone like to share where they were? Any particular sights or sounds? Any surprises? When could a mental vacation come in handy? (Trying to fall asleep at night or when you are bored and waiting for something.) When is it not a good idea to take a mental vacation? (When you should be paying attention or working.)

Variation:

Rather than letting the students pick a place, vividly describe a scene—the sounds of waves on a beach, seagulls overhead, the feel of sand under their feet. You can create a particular scene to introduce a story or an event in history.

Note: Remember that middle school students can be sensitive and very impressionable. Do not ask them to use this kind of visualization to imagine battle scenes or other violent or disturbing scenarios.

On The Edge

Objective: Get students' attention (can include discussion of force, motion, and friction)

Materials: One penny per student, desk or table top (smooth, flat surface with an edge), paper and pencil to keep score

Number of People: Any number

Time: 5–10 minutes

Directions: You can start or end this activity with a discussion about objects in motion, force, and friction. Divide the students into groups of three or four and have each group gather around a flat desk top. Tell students that they will take turns sliding their pennies across the desk, trying to get the pennies to stop as near to the edge as possible. Students can flick the pennies with their fingers or give the pennies a push, but they must let go of the pennies within the first three inches from the starting edge. Let each student slide his or her penny a couple of times to get a feel for the amount of force needed.

When the game starts, students take turns sliding the penny toward the edge (leave the penny where it stops—or pick it up off the floor if it goes over). If one penny hits another one and both pennies stay on the desk, their final spot is wherever they stop. If someone knocks another penny over the edge, but her penny stays on the desk, she remains in the game and the penny knocked off is out. If someone knocks another penny over the edge, but his also goes over the edge, the penny that was knocked off goes back to its original spot, and the one that did the knocking is out. After all three or four players have gone, the one closest to the edge for that round gets a point.

Have students take turns going first, second, third, and fourth so that the same person doesn't go first or last each time (this increases the fairness of having an opportunity to hit another penny). The student who went first the first round goes second the second round (the person who went second goes third, the person who went third goes first if there are three people.)

Play until someone gets 5 points (or 3 points or 10 points, depending on time limit).

Variations:

- Instead of using pennies, students can make little folded paper "footballs" for this activity.
- You can make more elaborate shuffleboard rules for this game and give different points for landing in different zones on the surface you are using.

Pendulum Predictor

Objective: Get students' attention and have them think about "mind over matter"

Materials: A pendulum for each student (a washer on a 12" string works well); desk or table top

Number of People: Any number

Time: Approximately 10 minutes

Directions: Give each student a pendulum, instructing them to keep it on their desks until told to pick it up. Once everyone has one, have the students hold the end of the string in their dominant hand with their elbow on the desktop at about a 90-degree angle and the pendulum almost touching the desktop. (Students with longer or shorter arms will need to adjust where they hold the string.) Tell the students not to spin the pendulums around, or they will be taken away.

Tell the students to make sure that the washer isn't moving, and then, "Without moving your hands, fingers, or arms, look at the pendulum and think to yourself 'left to right, left to right' (or 'east to west'). Really concentrate and see what happens." For many students, the pendulum will start swinging from left to right. Tell the students to stop the pendulum by touching it to the desktop and then repeat the exercise, but this time, "Think to yourselves, 'forward and backward' (or 'north to south, north to south') and see what happens." The pendulums should start swinging that direction for most students. Tell the students to stop the pendulum and see if they can get it swinging in a circle by concentrating and thinking "circle, circle."

Now that they have their pendulums working, tell them you will ask it a few questions. Side to side means "no" (like shaking your head "no"); forward and backward means "yes" (like nodding). A circle means "maybe." Students hold their pendulums still; you ask a few factual yes/no questions, such as "Is today Monday?" or "Are we in Alaska?" Next, ask a few prediction questions, such as "Will the (sports team) win this weekend?" or "Will it snow/rain today?" or "Are you going to make good grades this quarter?"

Ask the students how they think the pendulum works. If no one guesses correctly, tell them that even though they can't feel it, tiny muscle movements are making the pendulum swing in a particular direction. The pendulum transfers the energy over a longer distance and serves to accentuate the muscle movements so that we can see them.

Variation:

Have students make a target on a piece of paper with the N, S, W, E points marked to make the effect more noticeable.

Notes:

Take care to debrief this activity so that it isn't "spooky." The use of pendulums is open to opinion, but a scientific vs. paranormal discussion isn't needed for this quick, fun activity.

Also ensure that students return all pendulums at the end of the exercise, and always keep students from spinning them wildly or zinging them through the air. We don't want to put anyone's eye out.

What Do You See?

Objective: Get students' attention and have them think "outside the box"

Materials: Optical illusion transparencies, overhead projector, screen, ruler

Number of People: Any number

Time: 10–15 minutes for the four optical illusions and activity

Directions: Project the image onto a screen or blank wall. Tell the students to look at it silently. Ask a few students to tell what they see.

Woman's face or saxophone player?	An old woman or a young woman?	How many legs does the elephant appear to have?	Which line is the longest?

Have the students look at the first two transparencies until they can see both images. (You may need to point out where the nose is on each figure to help them find it.)

Have the students describe how the number of legs on the elephant seems to change as they look at it.

Use a ruler to show that the lines on the last illusion are all the same length.

Teaching Points:

What you see often depends on how you look at it. Some people can see things in different ways more quickly than others. It is hard to see something the same way again once you have seen it differently. Ask students how the activity might connect to "real life" (interactions with others, problem solving, etc.)

Variation:

"Floating Finger" Illusion: Have the students create their own optical illusion by holding their two index fingers in front of them, pointing at each other, about an inch apart, about 6" to 8" in front of their face. Have them soften their gaze to un-focus their vision and see if they can see a finger floating in the middle. (After they find one, they can add the other fingers to make four float.) Some students can see this right away; some take a long time to see it, if at all.

Woman's face or saxophone player?

An old woman or a young woman?

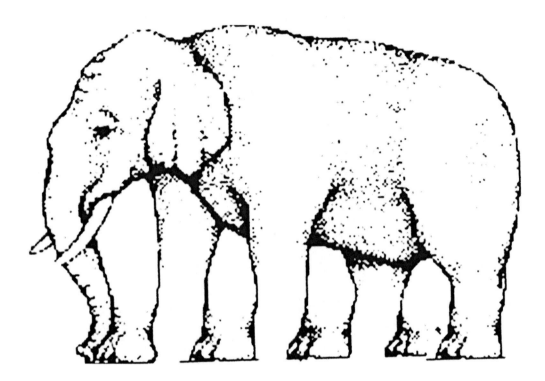

How many legs does the elephant appear to have?

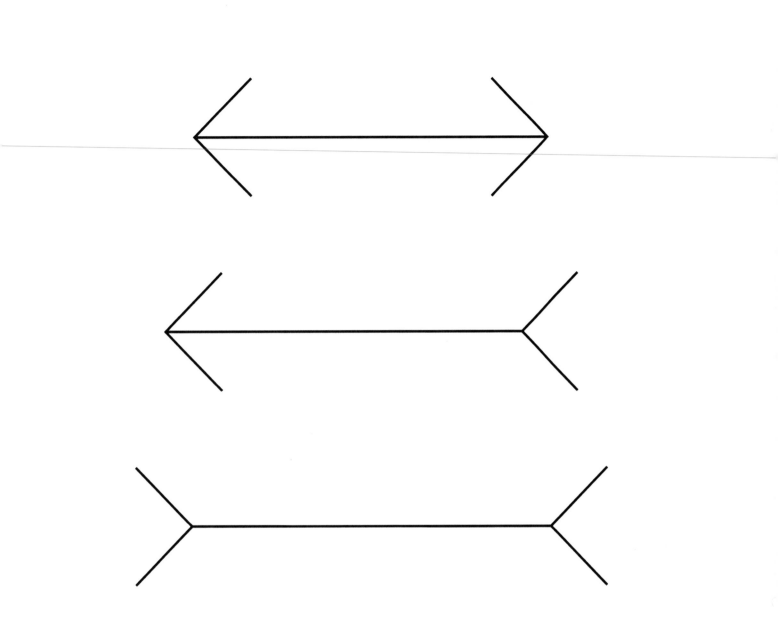

Which line is the longest?

Tell and Draw

Objective: To practice communication skills (clear instructions and careful listening)

Materials: Simple line drawings (samples follow); whiteboard, chalkboard, or paper; and markers

Number of People: Do in pairs or in a large group, with a "teller" and "drawer" in front of the group

Time: 3–5 minutes per drawing

Directions: Briefly introduce the class to the importance of clear communication when giving someone directions (how to do something, how to find a particular location). Ask for a volunteer to give directions (the "teller") and a volunteer to follow the directions (the "drawer").

The drawer goes to the board (or flipchart) and the teller stands with his back to the drawer. Give the teller a picture to describe to the drawer. Have a second copy to show the rest of the class while the teller is describing. The drawer cannot turn around and look. The teller must tell the drawer what to draw, without using parts of the actual object. For example, if the picture is of a house, the teller can say, "Draw a large square with a smaller rectangle in the center, touching the bottom line of the square." He cannot say, "Draw a door in the square."

After the teller has finished the directions, he can look at the results and show the drawer the original picture. There usually are some very strange pictures on the board, and the rest of the class usually laughs as they see what is happening compared to the target drawing.

The teller and drawer then pick students to take their places for another round with another picture.

Teaching Points:

Have students share ideas about how best to clarify directions. Talk about situations and jobs in which this skill is very important (e.g., following a recipe, controlling air traffic). Discuss how we often talk with our hands and how communicating is harder when you can't see the other person.

Variations:

- For more participation, make enough copies of each picture (after you demonstrate with the first one) so that partners can take turns being the teller and drawer. Put each picture in a small folder made of construction paper and have the teller hold it so that the drawer can't see the picture (this is difficult in small rooms). Keep the same partners for a few pictures, then rotate to new partners.

- Have one person in each pair draw her own picture and describe it to her partner.

Note: If students do their own drawings, you may need to remind them that the drawings need to be school-appropriate.

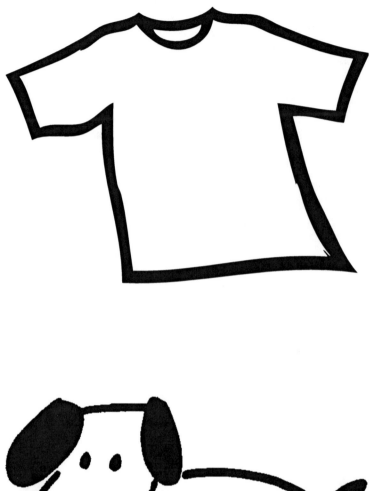

Teambuilding, Teamwork, and Collaborative Learning

Many middle schools use team names, colors, mottos, and competitions to develop camaraderie and a sense of belonging within grade level teams. Large middle schools even have more than one team within each grade level. Although middle school students enjoy competition, no one wants to be in a situation in which they cause their team to lose, whether by missing the final shot or giving the wrong answer in a Jeopardy game. Schools can certainly use competition between classes and grades for good causes, such as trying to bring in the most canned goods for the school food drive. School leaders need to create opportunities for the whole school to be viewed as a team and to ensure that the culture does not become divisive.

When perceived as fair, classroom competitions are fun because everyone has a chance to help their team, and there are many opportunities over the course of the year to be a winner. If games are fast-paced and students are in different groupings at different times, there isn't such a focus on winners and losers. There are many ways to increase teamwork so that one student doesn't get all the credit for the victory or full blame for the defeat. For example, during whiteboard races, students may be allowed to pass off the marker to a teammate if they don't know an answer. The teacher's interactions with students also help set the tone. ("You both are correct, but the gold team finished just a second ahead.")

There are lots of ways to divide a class into teams—counting off, passing out cards (Uno cards of different colors or standard playing cards using the different suits or numbers), drawing names from a hat, January through June birthdays vs. July through December. Having some "boys vs. girls" competitions can work well in middle school if the numbers are fairly even and the activity does not involve a skill that may be biased toward one of the sexes at this age (fine motor coordination vs. upper body strength). If you have a number of special needs students in your class, make sure your method of dividing into teams is fair and inclusive.

One method I never use for dividing into teams is picking "team captains" and letting those students choose sides. No matter how well the participants treat each other, it still doesn't feel good to be the last one picked. Even if you have the captains pick two students at a time, as I have seen some teachers do, being one of the last two picked doesn't feel much better.

Another word of caution concerning teams: Since the teams for these activities are temporary, don't let them spend a lot of time arguing about a team name for the race or activity. Middle school students will vehemently lobby for the name of their favorite sports team or come up with some very strange names that their teammates do not like. To speed things up, you can have some default names, like "Left Side" and "Right Side" (or North vs. South or East vs. West), depending on which area of the room the team is on.

Keep in mind that the purpose of these activities is to increase a sense of community and teamwork. If you are getting verbal and nonverbal cues that particular students or groups are feeling alienated, the class may need more work at the getting-acquainted level or with establishing class norms.

I designed the first four lesson plans (Class Constitution, Class Flag or Coat of Arms, Class Fight Song, and the first of the Circle-Up Activities) for the whole class to work together toward a common goal. The seven lessons that follow (Simple Relays, Tallest Tower, Mind Field, etc.) are geared toward competition between teams in the class, and the final six activities involve collaborative learning.

Twenty-first century learning skills. These activities provide students the opportunity to practice those 21st century skills that will make our young adolescents competitive in the global community. With some of the previous activities under their belts, they can practice respectful behavior, acknowledge different learning styles and values, and practice their critical thinking skills in their competitive and collaborative work.

Class Constitution

Objective: Create a set of class rules, rights, and responsibilities

Materials: Flipchart and markers; copy of the Preamble to the U.S. Constitution

Number of People: Any number

Time: 3 sessions, at least 15 minutes each

Directions:

Session 1: Ask the class what a constitution is. Use the U.S. Constitution as an example. Have students read the Preamble and discuss the purpose of the U.S. Constitution. Talk briefly about how we have federal laws, state laws, and city and county laws and ordinances. We also have school district regulations, which can be found in the Code of Conduct; and we have school rules, which can be found in the student handbook. The class will create a "class constitution" to help protect the rights and clarify the responsibilities of everyone in the classroom.

Divide the students into groups of four or five and have them brainstorm some things that should go in the class constitution. Assign one person in each group to be the recorder; at the end of the time, collect the ideas from each group.

Session 2: After students get back into their groups, hand them their lists. Have them review what they have so far and see if they want to add anything. Next, each group shares something from its list to see if the item (or something like it) is on any other group's list. If it appears on more than one group's list, put it on the master list to consider. If it doesn't appear on any other group's list, ask the other groups if they would like to add it to the master list. Go around the room until all the groups have shared their ideas. Tell the students they will be working with the master list next time to write the class constitution.

Session 3: Using the master list that was created during Session 2, work with the students to prioritize the list and reword items in the positive ("do this" rather than "don't do that," for example). Work with the class to come up with a good introduction ("We, the students of room 101 ..." "We, the students of Mr./Ms. X's advisory class ... in order to have an awesome year, agree to the following ..."). After the wording has been revised and agreed upon, make a final copy for all the students to sign and hang it on the wall.

Variations:

- Students memorize the class constitution. Ask for volunteers to present it to the class for public speaking practice using as much expression as possible.
- Students make their own copies of the class constitution for their binders.

Class Flag or Coat of Arms

Objective: Create a visual representation of what the class values

Materials: Pencil, paper or flipchart, markers for draft, materials to make coat of arms or flag (construction paper or fabric), sample coat of arms or flags (either pictures or the real thing)

Number of People: Any number

Time: 3 sessions, at least 15 minutes each

Directions:

Session 1: Ask students if they know what a coat of arms is. Briefly discuss the purpose of a coat of arms and where they are found (e.g., homes, colleges, flags of countries). Ask if any students have a family coat of arms. Show a couple of examples and describe how different items on the coat of arms are symbols for particular qualities, like freedom and bravery. If students are making flags, have them discuss flags from different countries and what their symbols represent.

This session is a brainstorming session, so have the students generate a list of qualities that are important to them as a group (friendship, fun, learning). Write the list on the board or flipchart. (If they have previously created a set of class rules, you may want to refer to it and see what values they represent.) Then ask them for ideas on what image or symbol might represent each quality. Get a few ideas for each quality. Tell the students that next time they will work on a design.

Session 2: Review the list of qualities and possible visual representations. Depending on the size of the group, either work together to vote on what to include and create a design; or, break into smaller groups and have each group work on some ideas. Create a draft of the design(s).

Session 3: Review the draft, and see if anyone has any ideas for changes. Reach consensus on the design. (Can everyone support it?) Work together to create the coat of arms or flag, or nominate a few students to make it.

Variation:

Students can work on a design individually or in pairs, in class or at home. Then the class can vote on the best design or combine ideas from different designs, or they can make modifications to the best one.

Class Fight Song

Objective: Create a song representing the class values

Materials: Pencil, paper or flipchart, markers for draft, sample college fight songs

Number of People: Any number

Time: 3 sessions, at least 15 minutes each

Directions:

Session 1: Share some sample fight songs or school songs with the class. Talk about what they have in common.

Famous Examples:

Excerpt from Notre Dame fight song:	**Excerpt from Michigan fight song –**
Cheer, cheer for old Notre Dame,	Hail! to the victors valiant
Wake up the echoes cheering her name,	Hail! to the conqu'ring heroes
Send a volley cheer on high,	Hail! Hail! to Michigan
Shake down the thunder from the sky.	The leaders and best!
What though the odds be great or small	Hail! to the victors valiant
Old Notre Dame will win over all,	Hail! to the conqu'ring heroes
While her loyal sons are marching	Hail! Hail! to Michigan,
Onward to victory	The champions of the West!

Students brainstorm a list of qualities that are important to them as a group (friendship, fun, learning); write the list on the board or flipchart. (If they have previously created a set of class rules, you may want to refer to it and see what values they represent.) Have the students pick a tune they want to use for their song.

Session 2: Review the list of qualities. Students work together to write a class song.

Session 3: Review the draft and see if anyone has any ideas for changes. Reach consensus on the song lyrics (Can everyone support it?). Practice the song together. Sing it for another class.

Variation:

Students can work on a song individually or in pairs, in class or at home. Then the class can vote on the best lyrics, combine ideas from different lyrics, or make modifications to the best one.

Circle-Up Activities

Objective: For students to interact and work together

Materials: None; some space to play

Number of People: 10 or more

Time: 5–20 minutes (depending on activity, number of people, etc.)

Directions:

These activities range from low-risk body contact to higher-risk body contact. Before the activities, establish group norms for not hurting anyone and for "challenge by choice" (i.e., the right to sit out if anyone is uncomfortable with the activity).

Telegraph: Students stand in a circle and clasp hands. Tell them you are going to send a signal around the group, that they must wait for it, and then pass it on when it reaches them. You can be the leader or allow students to take turns being the leader. The leader gently squeezes a hand and waits for it to make it around the circle. When it makes it back to the leader, the leader says that the signal is coming back around and gently squeezes the hand on the other side and again waits for the signal to travel all the way around. For the next round, instead of a squeeze, start a "wave" with one hand and watch it go around the circle. Then send a wave in both directions and see where it meets. Tell the students they can let go of hands and "shake it out."

Debriefing questions: What would keep the signal from making it all the way around? How is this activity a metaphor for teamwork? What is meant by the expression "A chain is only as strong as its weakest link?"

Finger Catch: Students stand in a circle with their left palms up, holding their hands "flat as a pancake," and gently touching their right index fingers in the palm of the person to their right. Tell them that when you say the word that starts with a "g" and ends with an "o," they are to simultaneously remove their right fingers from the palm of the person on the right and try to capture the index finger of the person on their left. The leader says "ready" (pause, look to make sure that left palms are flat and right index fingers are in place), "set" (pause), "GO." See how many were captured. (Tell them to let go if they haven't yet.) Then students switch hands, with right palm up and left index finger in the palm to the left.

Human Knot: Students stand in a circle and grasp hands with two different people who are not standing next to them. Tell the students that they now need to untangle the knot and form a circle, without letting go of hands. (They can re-grasp hands to change position to keep from spraining a wrist, but they can't make any other changes to break the chain.) You may end up with two circles when they are untangled. To turn this into a competition (if you have enough students), divide them into two equal groups and form two knots. The first team to untangle wins. You can also do variations in which only one student or a few students are allowed to speak.

Notes:

Watch for rowdy or risky behavior. Most students do very well with these types of activities, especially if they are reminded that they will not be allowed to play if they don't follow the rules.

Use humor to break the ice (e.g., "Go ahead and hold hands. The person next to you won't give you cooties!").

Also, have hand sanitizer available after hand-holding activities, especially during cold and flu season.

Simple Relays

Objective: Students interact and work together

Materials: Varies per relay (balls, stuffed animals, hula hoop); space to play

Number of People: 12 or more (best for 20–30)

Time: 10–20 minutes

Directions:

Over, Under Relay: Divide the students into two equal groups (if there's an odd number, the leader can play, or one student sits out for each round). Line up the two teams parallel to each other; the leader hands the first person in each row a ball (or stuffed animal or other round or soft object), and the first person passes the object back over his head to the second person. The second person passes the ball under her legs to the third person. The Over, Under relay continues to the back of the line; the last person in the row runs up to the front and starts again. If someone drops the ball, he needs to pick it up, get back in line and pass it to the person behind. Note: If a girl is wearing a skirt or dress, she only passes overhead.

Variations Include:
If the ball drops, the whole team must start over. The first team to get their first person back to the front of the line wins. (If space is limited, you might need to reposition the line as the game proceeds, because the line tends to creep forward after each person if the others don't shuffle back a bit.)

Pitch and Catch Relay: Divide the students into two equal groups (if there's an odd number, the leader can play, or one student sits out for each round). Divide each team into two groups and have the groups face each other in two parallel lines. Give the first person in each of the two teams a ball and have them pass the ball to the person across from them. The first person in the line passes to the first person in the facing line; the first person in the facing line then throws the ball to the second person in the line facing her. Play continues with second to second, second to third, third to third, third to fourth, and back up the line until it returns to the first person. The first team to return the ball to the first person wins. If someone drops the ball, he needs to pick it up, get back in line, and pass it to the next person.

Variations Include:
If the ball drops the whole team must start over. Use jai alai rackets or lacrosse sticks for the pitch-catch. Hand the racket or stick to the next person, or give one per person if you have enough. Use a balloon or beach ball for a different dynamic.)

Hula Hoop Relay: Divide the students into two equal groups (if there's an odd number, the leader can play, or one student sits out for each round). The groups each form a circle and join hands. Two students in each of the teams let go of hands long enough to put a large hula hoop around one of their arms, and then reclasp hands. When the leader says "go," the students pass the hula hoop around the circle by stepping through the hoop and then passing over the next person's head, all without letting go of hands. The first team to get the hula hoop back to the starting point wins. Notes: Do not do this activity if there is a student who is too large to fit through the hula hoop.

Back-to-Back Relay: Two students hold a ball or balloon between their two backs and walk with their backs together until they deposit the item across a finish line. If they drop the item, they must go back to the beginning.

Tallest Tower

Objective: Students interact and work together to reach a goal; also has math, science, tech applications

Materials: Foam blocks, tape measure (or string and yardstick for measuring), stopwatch or clock with a second hand, flat surfaces for building

Number of People: 5–30

Time: 15–20 minutes

Directions: For small groups, competition can be between individuals or pairs. For large groups, break into teams of three to five people per team. (This activity is hard with more than five in a group, but it can be done to show the challenge of involving everyone in certain kinds of tasks.)

Give each team the same number of blocks by having each person on the team come and get x number of blocks (5 or 10, depending on the size of the group).

Rules: Set a time limit of 5–10 minutes for the teams to construct a tower. When a team is ready to be judged, have someone start the stopwatch or watch the clock—the tower must stand on its own for at least one minute while it is measured. Use a tape measure or string next to the tower, and do not touch the tower while measuring the height. If the tower falls before it has an official measure, the team may rebuild, as long as the time limit hasn't expired. If a team has not asked to have their tower measured before the time is up, then what they have at the end of the time will be measured. The team with the tallest tower wins.

Teaching Points:

Have the teams talk about risk vs. safety, height vs. stability, and speed vs. planning. Observe the groups and watch for leadership, conflict, and supportive roles.

Variations:

- If there is time, you can do another round or combine teams.
- Try a round without talking.
- Ask students to discuss what science or math principles apply (gravity, force, mass, angles).

Note: Rather than buying foam blocks, you may be able to find companies that routinely discard foam blocks used in packing.

Balloon Volleyball and Balloon Relay

Objective: Students work together to achieve a goal

Materials: Balloon (extra balloons, in case it pops), paper banner, string or tape for net; can be played inside

Number of People: 10–30

Time: 10–20 minutes

Directions:

Balloon Volleyball: Depending on the size of the classroom and how much floor space you have, desks can either be moved back and a net set up (paper banner, string, or masking tape strip across the room), or students can stay in their desks, and one side of the room plays against the other side of the room.

Rules: Decide if regular volleyball rules apply (rotate servers, no more than three hits on a side, etc.), or if you want to make your own rules. To get more students involved, rules can include that each side must hit the balloon at least three times (three different people) before it goes to the other side. If the balloon touches the floor (wall, ceiling, desks), then it is out and the other team gets a point. First side to score 15 points (or 5 or 10 points, depending on time limit and the type of rules) wins.

Variations:

- Play a silent version: anyone who speaks is out.
- Students can only hit the balloon with their heads, or elbows, or a rolled up piece of paper.

Balloon Relay: Students on each team form a line and pass a balloon using only the eraser-end of two pencils. (Either use just two pencils and have the students pass the balloon and the pencils OR have each student hold two pencils and take just the balloon from the person.) If the balloon drops, they need to pick it up and start it at the beginning. The first team to get their balloon to the finish line (or in a tub, basket, or bucket) wins.

Variations:

- For a longer game, each team can pass more balloons.
- To be fair, you may want to supply new, unsharpened pencils so the pencils are all the same length.

Beanbag Toss

Objective: Students work together to achieve a goal

Materials: Beanbags, paper, or sheet; target or board with holes; some space to play

Number of People: Any number

Time: 15–20 minutes

Directions: You can make beanbags by putting beans in a plastic zip bag, placing the bag in a sock (use the short anklet style in a kids size), and sewing it shut; or use a longer sock, close it with a twist-tie, and fold the open end of the sock back over the beanbag. If you have five on a team, it helps to have at least five beanbags so that each person can toss one. If you don't have enough beanbags, keep score as students toss, and then toss the beanbags back to them to be used again.

You can make a wooden target with holes from plywood or other sturdy material. Or, make a target from a large roll of paper, or an old sheet. The size of the target depends on the size of the bean bags and the amount of space in which you have to play. The number of points per circle or hole can vary depending on how complex you want to make the scoring, especially with multiplication or other math variations.

Divide students into teams; four or five per team works well. Set up a board with holes cut in it. Holes can be of different sizes, with smaller holes worth more points. Alternatively, put a paper target on the floor, with the smaller inner rings of the target worth more points. This version is like a combination of horseshoes and darts.

The person tossing stands on a designated spot (a line on the floor, for example). Either have members from two teams alternate tossing and keep track of the score, or have one team toss their beanbags (one at a time) and add up their score before the next team goes.

Variations:

- *Timed Version:* Give the team a certain number of beanbags and tell them they have two minutes to score as many points as they can. Options: They all have to toss. Or, they pick one or two people to toss, and the other people are scorekeepers and relay the beanbags back to the people tossing. Give the next team the same number of beanbags and the same time limit.

- *Variation on a Variation:* Give both teams the same time limit, but give one team more beanbags than the other. (This could lead to a discussion about imbalance of power, some having more resources than others.)

- *Multiplication Version:* Multiply each of the scores instead of adding them.

Mind Field

Objective: Students work together to achieve a goal

Materials: Carpet squares or masking tape, clipboard, grid to draw route, paper to keep track of "kabooms," stopwatch; space to play

Number of People: best with 10–24

Time: 5–20 minutes (for two rounds)

Directions: Place carpet squares in a 4 x 4, 4 x 5, 4 x 6, 5 x 5, 5 x 6, or 6 x 6 grid, with squares touching. Alternatively, make a grid on the floor using masking tape (wide blue painter's tape is easier to see).

The leader draws a safe route on a grid. Use overhead transparency markers to reuse grids placed inside a page-protector. Each step on the route must connect, sideways, forward, or diagonally. For more complicated routes, use backward steps. A square cannot be used more than once. Players must step on the squares in the correct order, so a square might not be safe until the one before it has been used. In the example below, players cannot go from 3 to 5 until they have stepped on 4. The leader tells players how many steps it takes to get across the field, and if there are any backward moves.

1				
	2	3		
		4	5		8
			6	7	

Divide the group into two teams; they flip a coin or play "rock, paper, scissors" to see which team goes first. The winner of the toss usually lets the other team go first so that they can learn from other team's mistakes and know what time they have to beat. The team crossing the "mind field" gathers on one end of the field. The other team holds the clipboard at the opposite end. The leader says "go," and a student starts the stopwatch. When a player tries a square, the team with the clipboard says "safe" if it is the right square or "kaboom" if it isn't and puts a tally mark on the side of the grid (or another student can keep track of kabooms on a separate piece of paper). Each player proceeds until he or she gets kaboomed. Only one player is on the field at a time. Everyone has a turn before anyone can try again. Team members can give verbal reminders or suggestions, but they can't touch the field. When someone gets to the final safe square and steps off the field, the timer stops the watch and records the time and number of kabooms. The leader then makes another route, with the same number of steps of similar difficulty for the other team. The team that makes it across the field with the shortest time and fewest kabooms wins. (Teams tie if each one wins a category.) Talking Points include: learning from others' mistakes, supporting team members, paying attention, and following directions.

Variation: Put numbers on the squares and make the route across the field a math concept (even numbers connected, only prime numbers are safe, only square roots are safe.)

Flying Carpet or Flying Saucer Relay

Objective: Students interact and work together to reach a goal (also good for burning off some energy)

Materials: Carpet squares or paper plates, construction paper and tape for variations; space to play (gym or outside)

Number of People: Best for 10–30

Time: 15–20 minutes (depending on number of rounds); allow two class periods if students create paper plate version

Directions:

Individual Version: Each student has a carpet square and starts with his foot on the line at the end of the basketball floor or against the fence outside. When the leader says "go," he throws his carpet square (flying-disc fashion) and chases after it. He picks it up and throws it again until he gets to the other side (far wall or other fence). Then he touches the wall/fence and repeats the throwing and running back to the start. Important rule: students must throw from where the carpet landed. They can back up a few steps and take a running start to their throw, but they must not run with the carpet beyond where it has landed. The first person back to the starting line with the carpet wins.

Paired Version: Same activity, but two students share a carpet square and take turns throwing. Both run after the carpet and stay together, OR one student waits at the far side while the other one throws and then returns the carpet square on the second half of the relay.

Team Version: Depending on the size of the playing field, teams of 3 to 5 can share a carpet square and take turns throwing.

Variations:

- For an inside version, use paper plates instead of carpet squares. Individuals or teams should label or decorate their plates so that they get their own when playing.
- Science/Technology Variation: Teams can be given two paper plates, some tape, and two pieces of construction paper to modify their plates with the goal of making them fly better. Teams construct the flying objects and test them, then begin the relay. Discuss the principles behind the improved aerodynamics.

Note: This activity is pretty rough on the carpet squares. They may not withstand too many relays.

Pirate Pick Up

Objective: Students interact and work together to achieve a goal (also has math and science applications)

Number of People: 4 or more (best with 12–24)

Time: 5–20 minutes (depending on number of items and rounds)

Materials: "Pirate hook" (shower drain piece, heavy string, a hook, nut); items to rescue; box, or blanket; stopwatch or clock with second hand; space to play

Directions: Here is one way to make a pirate hook for this activity. Cut as many 10-foot lengths of heavy string as number of holes in the outside ring of the shower drain (about 12 to 14 in most). Fold the string in half; put the closed end through an outside hole of the drain and pull the two tails of the string through the loop to secure it. This will give you two 5-foot lengths of string. (String can be slightly longer or shorter, but if many students are playing, they need about 5 or 6 feet of string so there is room for everyone to stand in a circle.) Tie a knot about 6 inches from the end of each of the strings. (You should have twice as many 5-foot lengths of string as there are holes.) Put the hook through the center hole of the metal drain and secure it with the nut.

Scatter 5 to 10 items that need to be "rescued" on the playing field (or on a large blue tarp to simulate water; add the rule that no one can step "in the water"). The items must have some sort of surface that can be hooked, and they must be light enough to be picked up without breaking the string.

Each student takes the end of a string and must keep his or her hand on the knot; that is, students can't reach down the string with their other hand or wrap the string around their hands to make it shorter. (If you have more strings than people, some students will have more than one. If you have more people than strings, some will sit out; or, if you're doing one of the variations below, have the "extra" students give orders or guide a blindfolded person.) The leader says "go" and times how long it takes to pick up the items with the hook and deposit them in a box or tub, or on a blanket. If an item drops, it must be picked up with the hook again. Tell them how long it took and let them set a time goal for the next round.

Teaching Points:

Discuss what is needed for everyone to be able to pull together to accomplish the goal. Discuss math and science principles (angles, force, etc.).

Variation:

- No talking for one round or only one or two people can talk. Some people can be blindfolded.
- Competition: Divide into teams and take turns picking up the items; see which team can pick up the items in the shortest time.

How Many Uses?

Objective: Students interact and work together to practice creative thinking skills

Materials: Paper, pens or pencils, a bag of ordinary objects (shoe box, straw, safety pin, car key)

Number of People: 5–30

Time: 10–20 minutes (activity can be repeated, using different objects)

Directions: Tell the students they are going to practice creative thinking. Each student takes out a piece of paper and a pen or pencil. Tell them you will take an object out of the bag, and they will list as many uses as they can for the object. Start with the most obvious intended use for the object, and then think about other ways to use it. Hint: most things could also serve as a paperweight, to keep papers from blowing away.

Give the students a time limit (3 to 5 minutes). Call time and ask who has written more than five uses. Then ask how many have more than six, seven, eight, etc., until you find out who has the most. Have students share their answers and decide whether or not they are reasonable. Their ideas must be something the object can be on its own and within reason. For example, a shoe box could be a home for a turtle, but it could not reasonably be a good radio.

Now the students will get into teams and put their heads together to come up with a list of uses for another object. Divide the class into groups of four to six students. Try to have some space between the groups so that they don't hear each other's ideas. Have one person from each team volunteer to take notes, or have the teammates take turns with each person writing down two or three ideas and then passing the list to the next person. Take another object out of the bag and say "go." At the end of the time limit, find out which team has the most ideas. Have the teams share their ideas out loud and take any off the list that you or the class judges as an unreasonable use.

Teaching Points:

Was it easier with the second object, after you were warmed up? Did someone else's idea give you an idea? Talk about how good ideas feed each other. How would this activity help in the work world?

Variation:

You can provide the actual object for each group to handle while brainstorming (one shoe box per group, etc.) This can be distracting, but if students are able to stay on task, being able to hold the object usually results in more ideas.

The Judge

Objective: Practice and reinforce basic skills through repetition

Materials: Flashcards with questions or problems on one side and answers on the other (preferably an odd number); desks in groups of 3

Number of People: 3 or more (best with 12–24)

Time: 15–20 minutes or more (depends on number of rounds)

Directions: Decide if you want to have a mix of cards at each station or divide the cards to focus on one skill at each station.

Students work in groups of three, with one judge and two contestants. (Note: If class size isn't divisible by three, you can have one or two groups of four, with one judge and three contestants.) The judge sits on one side, opposite the two contestants. The judge holds the flash cards with the problem/question sides facing the contestants and the answer sides facing her; the contestants shouldn't see the answer until the judge shows it to them. The contestants race to see who can say the correct answer first. (You can also have contestants write down the answer on paper or individual whiteboards.) The judge hands the winner the card.

If neither contestant answers correctly, the judge shows them the answer and places the card back in the stack to be tried again. If both contestants say the correct answer at the same time, the judge puts the card down, and the contestant who wins the next card gets that card as well. The contestant with the most cards at the end of the round wins and becomes the judge. (It is best to have an odd number of cards at each station to avoid a tie.) The judge moves to the next group and becomes a contestant.

You can play this game in one of two ways:

a. Slow: Wait until each group finishes its stack before having everyone move on.

b. Fast: As soon as one group finishes, the judge for that group yells "Done!" (or rings a bell in the middle of the room, flashes the lights, or makes some other signal to stop). Everyone immediately stops and counts cards to find out who becomes the judge.

As soon as one person wins at every station ("Around the World"), the game is over; or you can stop when time is up.

Variations:

- Learn vocabulary words in a foreign language.
- Review math, science, language arts, and social studies concepts.
- Learn musical notation and vocabulary.

Notes: This game can get very loud and wild, but students are usually on task. Keep reminding them to quiet down and not to grab for the cards. Ask the judges to hold the cards still until voices are back down. If someone gets too wild, have him or her sit out a round.

Memory Match

Objective: Review anything that can be paired (terms and definitions, states and capitals, math problems and answers)

Materials: One set of memory cards per pair of students; desk or table top

Number of People: Any number

Time: 10–20 minutes (more if students make the cards)

Directions: Make pairs of cards for items to be reviewed. The number of cards students will match should fit on a desktop. You should have a minimum of 20 cards (for 10 items to be matched); students will lay these out in a grid of 4 rows and 5 columns. Other grid possibilities include these: 24 cards (4 x 6 grid); 30 cards (5 x 6 grid); 36 cards (6 x 6 grid).

The teacher can make the cards on the computer, and copy and cut a classroom set (one group of cards for each pair of students); or students can make the cards as part of the review. Half of a 3" x 5" index card is a good size (2.5" x 3"), so students can use one index card for the two cards to be matched. (Make sure they don't use a marker or pen that will show through the card.)

Here are examples of items students might match: one card has a term and the other card has the definition, one card has a picture and the other card has the name, one card has a state and the other has its capital, one card has a math problem and the other has the answer.

When it is time for the game to begin, have the students work in pairs. Shuffle one set of cards and put them, blank side up, in a grid on the desktop. Students take turns turning over two cards to see if they match. If they match, the student keeps the cards in a stack on his side. If they don't match, the student turns them back over. (Option: If a student gets a match, she gets another turn.) Take turns until all cards have been matched. Students count their cards, and the student with the most cards wins.

Teacher circulates to make sure the matches are correct.

Variations:

Play with more than two people using the set of cards, especially if there are a lot of cards and a large playing surface.

Rock, Paper, Scissors Variations

Objective: Students interact and practice math concepts

Materials: None required; paper and pencil to keep score, optional

Number of People: 3 or more

Time: 5–20 minutes

Directions: Divide the students into groups of three. If the class is not divisible by 3, one or two people will need to rotate into the game.

Tell the students this game is like "Rock, Paper, Scissors." However, instead of saying "Rock, paper, scissors," they say "odd one wins" as they hit their open palms with their fists (on "odd" and "one"). Then on the word "wins," they show 0 (fist) or up to five fingers. The point always goes to the person who doesn't match the other two in terms of holding up an odd or even number of fingers. For example, if two people show an even number of fingers or a fist (0, 2, or 4) and one person shows an odd number of fingers (1, 3, or 5), then the one person showing the odd number of fingers gets a point. Similarly, if two people show an odd number of fingers (1, 3, or 5) and one person shows an even number of fingers or a fist (0, 2, or 4), then the one person (the one with the even number of fingers) gets a point. It is a tie if all three people show 0, 2, or 4 or all three people show 1, 3, or 5. The first person to score 5 points (or 10, depending on how long you want to play) wins.

Variations:

- *Around the World:* Arrange the groups in a circle and have the winner from each round move on to the next group. (This will take some timing finesse if a group needs to wait on another group to break a tie.) To make the game move faster, winners can move on to the next group after winning 1 point or 3 points, instead of 5. The first person to get back to their original position in the circle wins.

- *Do the Math:* You can do this variation with 2, 3, 4, or 5 people. On the first two fist pounds say "Do the," and on the word "math," show 1 to 5 fingers.

- *Addition Version:* The first person to add all the fingers and say the correct sum wins.

- *Multiplication Version:* The first person to multiply the fingers and say the correct sum wins.

Story Cards

Objective: Students work together to create a story   **Number of People:** 5–25

Materials: Story cards, flipchart paper and marker (or paper and pencil)   **Time:** 20 minutes

Directions: Create your own story cards, using keywords and/or pictures. You can get pictures from magazines, old calendars, and so on; you also can find clip art on the Internet or from other sources. It's best if the story cards are on the same size paper (3"x 5" card or half-sheet of paper).

Small-Group Story Telling: Give each person a card (or two to three cards, depending on the size of the group). Tell the students to form groups of three to five students and put all their story cards together to create a story. (You can add a rule that they can choose not to include one or two cards in the story.) Have one student from each group be the scribe. Students can either read the stories to the group (If you're out of time, read the stories in the next session.), or post their stories for the students to read on their own.

Whole-Group Story Telling: Have the students sit in a circle so that they can see and hear each other. Give each of them one or more story cards. Ask for a volunteer to be the scribe. (The scribe can have a card and contribute to the story, or she can just record.)

Pick someone to start the story. You can either go around the circle in order, or you can have students add to the story by raising their hands and adding a line or two when they think their contributions will fit well. Here's an example:

> First student: One summer day, a farmer decided to build a new barn.

> Second student: He needed the barn for his new hippo. He had rescued the hippo from a frozen pond.

After everyone has added his or her lines to the story, someone reads the story from beginning to end.

Variations:

- Students can put the picture cards on a poster with the story, or they can create a book.
- Use one of the stories to practice editing. Organize it into paragraphs. Fix run-on sentences. Add connections to improve flow.
- Without knowing what the activity entails, students can create the story cards before it begins.

Who Am I?

Objective: Students interact and practice asking good questions to find an answer

Materials: Slips of paper and masking tape (or self-adhesive labels or name tags), pen or marker

Number of People: 5 or more

Time: 10–20 minutes

Directions: Write the name of a famous person and a short description of him or her on a piece of paper, label, or name tag (e.g., George Washington, first U.S. President). You can specify a category, such as Famous Americans or Modern Celebrities or Fictional Characters. Have enough names for each member of the class. Tape a name on the back of each student, without him or her seeing the name.

Have students ask each other "yes" or "no" questions to try to guess who they are. Questions they could ask might include "Am I a man?" "Am I still alive?" "Did I play sports?" "Was I in government?" Students can ask only two questions of any person, so that they get around to several students. In smaller groups, you can increase the number of questions they ask each person.

When a student guesses his identity, he moves the name tag to his front and continues answering others' questions, until all students have figured out their identities.

Teaching Points:

Ask the students what kinds of questions were most helpful in narrowing down and figuring out their identities. Did they have a strategy? Did they start with the general and move to the more specific?

Variations:

- Turn this into a competition by seeing who figures out his or her identity first or who can do it with the fewest number of questions (Students must keep track of how many questions they have asked.)

- Instead of "Who am I?" make this activity "What am I?" and use vocabulary words from science, geography, geometry, Spanish, art, or music to review a unit.

Notes:

It is possible that some students may not have heard of one of your examples of famous people, and it is challenging to create a list that is equally difficult for all students to guess. If you randomly pick each student's identity from the stack, they just get the luck of the draw.

If you use famous people or characters, try to get a good mix of male and female figures and a wide range of ethnic diversity.

Resources and Suggested Reading

Jack Berckemeyer. (2009). *Managing the madness.* Westerville, OH: National Middle School Association.

Richard DuFour, Rebecca DuFour, Robert Eaker, & Gayle Karhanek. (2004). *Whatever it takes: How professional learning communities respond when kids don't learn.* Bloomington, IN: Solution Tree Press.

Eric Jensen. (2009). *Super teaching,* fourth edition. Thousand Oaks, CA: Corwin. (www.jensenlearning.com)

Eric Larsen & William M. Timpson. (2001). *The discovery program: Essential skills for teachers and students.* Longmont, CO: Sopris West.

Doug Lemov. (2010). *Teach like a champion: 49 techniques that put students on the path to college.* San Francisco: Jossey-Bass.

Robert J. Marzano, Debra J. Pickering, & Jane E. Pollock. (2001). *Classroom instruction that works.* Alexandria, VA: Association for Supervision and Curriculum Development. (www.marzanoresearch.com/site/default.aspx)

John Perricone. (2005). *Zen and the art of public school teaching.* Frederick, MD: Publish America. (www.johnperricone.com/index.html)

Jill Spencer. (2008). *Everyone's invited! Interactive strategies that engage young adolescents.* Westerville, OH: National Middle School Association.

Rick Wormeli. (2001). *Meet me in the middle: Becoming an accomplished middle level teacher.* Portland, ME & Westerville, OH: Stenhouse & National Middle School Association. (www.nmsa.org/store)

CPSIA information can be obtained at www.ICGtesting.com
Printed in the USA
BVOW051411160712

294964BV00006B/1/P